GRIEF SUCKS

LETTERS TO DADDY

Becky Holland

GRIEF SUCKS
LETTERS TO DADDY

BY

Becky Holland

© Copyright 2023 by Printed Page Publishers - All rights reserved.

It is not legal to reproduce, duplicate, or transmit any part of this document in either electronic means or printed format. Recording of this publication is strictly prohibited.

Dedication

In memory of my daddy, James Colonel Holland,
He would've understood why.
September 28, 1933 – August 16, 2023

Introduction

Grief is normally defined as *"deep sorrow, especially that caused by someone's death."* The Cleveland Clinic took the definition of grief a step further, and I like the way they went with it.

From their website, www.clevelandclinic.org, we read, *"Grief is the experience of coping with loss. Most of us think of grief as happening in the painful period following the death of a loved one. But grief can accompany any event that disrupts or challenges our sense of normalcy or ourselves. This includes the loss of connections that define us. You may grieve the loss of: A friend, family member, partner or pet; A marriage, friendship or another form of kinship; Your home, neighborhood or community; Your job or career; Financial stability; A dream or goal; Good health; Your youth or fertility."*

Self-help books out there about grief talk about the five stages of grief as if these were rules. Elizabeth Kubler-Ross described the five stages in **"On Death and Dying,"** her book which was published in 1969. Stages include *denial, anger, bargaining, depression and acceptance*. Other books add in the types of grief, like, **anticipatory grief** – grieving before they actual loss, **abbreviated grief** – you move quickly through the stages of the grieving process, **delayed grief** – you feel the emotions of grief for a long time, **inhibited grief** – when you don't process the emotions, **cumulative grief** – grieving multiple losses at once and **collective grief** – where you are grieving as a group.

Each one of those books and the credentialed people that write them give amazing explanations and wonderful ways to get through grief. Their answers are based on tons of scholarly research (allegedly), and some say they have done a lot of interviews of people processing through grief. There are even some spiritual books about grief – those with actual scriptures quoted I tend to believe more than others where folks try to make the scriptures fit their needs.

There is no one size fits all solution or fit for grief and how to handle grieving – no matter how many stages there have been found to be. As I was looking into writing this book, I found someone else had decided there were seven stages of grief. We all experience grief differently.

In writing this book, I have to say, I don't have a solution or an answer or a method for you. The way I see it is simple. Grief sucks. Losing someone you love sucks. It hurts worse than a flu shot, and poison ivy remedy shot combined. God will get you through it. He will, I promise, and there is a ton of scripture to prove that.

But it still hurts to lose someone, especially someone who has been a strong presence in your life since the day you were born … like your daddy.

My daddy was a month shy of turning 90 when he died. I was there at least 20 minutes before he passed away. James Colonel Holland was truly a unique and strong presence in the lives of those that knew him.

What do I have to say to you that could help you anymore than all the self-help gurus haven't already said? Not much, except to share with you my own personal experience, and let you gather your own meaning from our story. You may not find a meaning, but maybe you will find some comfort or peace in reading it. Anne Wilson wrote in her book, **"My Jesus,"** *"Whatever you are feeling, God can handle it--all of it. The tears, screams, and questions. God invites you to let Him tend to your heart."*

I will say this. There is one thing I would like to tell you. The stages of grief really aren't rules. There is no time limit. Don't let anyone tell you different.

My mom asked me what we were going to do without Daddy the other day. I said, "Keep on living."

Oh, and dear reader, it is **OK to cry.**

Much Love,
Becky

PART I: Who Was He?

I get a weekly email from a writer's website that includes a list of creative writing prompts. One this week caught my attention. "Write a story starring an octogenarian who's more than meets the eye."

In September of 1933, a loud slap and a cry was the signal that Tullie and Lois Holland had delivered a baby- their oldest, a son, whom they named James Colonel Holland. A few years later, his brother joined the family, and it was just the two boys and their parents living the simple life in rural middle Georgia.

As a child, James was normal – played outside, went to school, played outside some more and went to church. Back in those days, the only devices one had to communicate with was the party line, or their own two feet – that's when you would walk down the road to your grandparents for a visit or next door to your neighbor's for a cup of sugar. There was no app and no texting.

James loved that and loved hanging out with the boys from the neighborhood – a lot of whom he was related to in some form or fashion. He loved to watch the trains go through the community, and even got to ride a few – depending on the mood of the conductor, and his mother.

One of the things James was good at as a child and teenager was playing baseball. He was a catcher and a short stop for school and community teams, and oh, yeah, just when playing baseball out in someone's yard. People wanted him to play on their team.

The one team though that James gladly served on was God's team. He became a Christian at an early age, and sometime, after marrying the love of his life, Gerry, James felt the call to preach. He attended East Texas Baptist College in Marshall, Texas, and was later ordained as a Baptist minister at Second Baptist Church in Marshall. He pastored for a short time in several rural churches in middle Georgia and east Texas. Even after leaving the active pastorate, James and Gerry, and their family stayed involved in the ministries of their home churches as Sunday School leaders and more.

People always wanted James to be on their "team…" including at jobs he had in Robins Air Force Base, Darco (Marshall, Texas) and with his own plumbing/electrical/HVAC contracting company, Holland Mechanical Service.

His honesty, exceptional work ethic and resourcefulness caught the eye of all his employers, and people who wanted him to "wire" or "cool" their house.

James had many talents and gifts that folks didn't know he had – like his love of working with his hands and building things to his love of learning. He built computers, and even rebuilt one at the beginning of 2023 at the age of 89.

James passed away yesterday after an extended illness. He was 89.

He certainly was an octogenarian who was 'more than meets the eye.'

I should know because he was Dad to me and my brother and sisters.

Signed, *Becky*

Chapter One: The Day You Left

Dear Daddy,

August 16, 2023, is the day you left us to meet Jesus in Heaven. It was sometime in the morning - about 20-30 minutes after I left after visiting you – when you fell into your heavenly, peaceful sleep.

You were asleep for most of the time I was there, and we didn't really talk. You would look at me and acknowledge my presence with a nod. The certified nursing assistant came in and said you had asked for me so that we could be there to visit.

Funny thing about that. No one called from the nursing home to tell us. Donna was sitting at the table with Mom, and she said, "One of us should go up there."

I didn't say anything or ask questions. I just got up from my chair at the computer and went to the room to get dressed. I don't remember saying bye. I am sure I did. I just remember going to my car and seeing that one of my final sunflowers – which I had thought had died due to the heat – blooming.

When I got to the nursing home, all the pictures and cards I had hung on the board had fallen to the floor. They were pictures of your family, and cards from a plethora of folks who love you and care for you. You like the big word? Plethora?

You taught me that word you know. I remember reading something you wrote, and you made me look it up. Plethora is defined as an *"excessive or large amount of something."* You had a bunch of cards, and I have to say, I had a plethora of thoughts and emotions flowing through my brain and heart that day too.

It was hard seeing you as you were – so skinny and frail. You are Daddy – the provider, the strong one, the armchair philosopher and the leader of our home.

I remember sitting in that chair, and just staring at you as you lay on the nursing home bed. Your sheets were intertwined with your legs. Your breathing was labored somewhat, but you were still breathing. You always liked to say, "I am breathing with purpose."

Knowing now what I know, I am sure your purpose was preparing for the next journey you were about to take. My phone rang, and I answered it. My conversation was brief. When I hung up, you turned to me and said, "I didn't understand what you said."

I moved closer, and took your limp hand, and said, "It was someone on the phone … I love you, Daddy." You gave me a very slight, weakened smile, and turned your head. "Are you going to sleep?"

Your head nodded, and your eyes shut. I watched your chest to see it move with breaths. I remember watching for several minutes. I kissed you on your forehead and moved back to my chair.

I was not sure what to do next. That was odd for me. I texted Donna, and asked if I should come back, that you were sleeping. We were all going to come back together – Donna, Momma and me.

Her text was a simple yes.

I remember talking to your nurse, asking if you had a bath and ate. She said you had eaten, and she would check the bath schedule. I told her we would be back later, and turned back to your room to tell you I was going to get Mom and Donna. You were sleeping soundly.

I saw your chest go up and down.

It took me 15 minutes to get home. I made a stop at the gas station. When I arrived, Donna was on the phone, and Mom was getting ready to come see you.

As I was standing in the room, encouraging Mom, Donna stepped into my view, shook her head, and made a sign.

I knew what she was saying. You had died. I just stood there a minute, and distracted Mom with something while I followed Donna out of the room.

She was talking to the Hospice nurse. When she got off the phone, she told me what had happened. I could feel the tears, but at the same time, I didn't want to cry. We knew this was going to happen. You had been preparing me for the day that both you and Mom would die for the last 15 years, but most especially the last four, since I moved back to hang out with you guys while you aged appropriately.

"Death is just as an important part of life as being born is," you would say when I would cringe every time the topic was brought up. You would remind me that God was not just God when we were born, but also when we died.

And here we were. You had died. When we told Mom, we talked about you being in no pain, and how as a Christian, we knew where you were, and that we should celebrate your welcome into Heaven. (Maybe not in those words, but it was close.)

You would have been proud of Momma – she is a trooper.

We made it to the nursing home to see you before the funeral home came to take you away for your cremation.

They had you in bed with your Tri-County Monitor shirt on. I found your hat. Donna fixed it on your head.

We cried a bit, talked, and then left. Things had to be done, and we had calls to make.

At some point during the night, laying in the bed, I think it hit me. You had left us. What were we going to do without you?

I heard it as plain as day as if it was in your own voice in my head, "Keep going."

And that is what we are doing, Daddy. We are keeping on, keeping on.

Love, Becky

Chapter Two: The Day We Sold Your Old Truck

Dear Daddy,

In the mid-1980s, you brought home a Toyota truck. It was to be used for a work truck – to add to your "fleet" of three to four vehicles used for the heating and air conditioning and plumbing and electrical business you operated.

It became one of your favorite trucks. It was white with a little colored interior. Two people could fit – three if that third person was small. The back was always filled with tools and other needed equipment.

The truck had *your* smell. *Your smell* being the smell of work. I loved that smell. I remember one time you told me a story about how smells were nostalgic for you – especially crop season for peanuts. You said it reminded you of your growing up years – same went for cotton being binned.

Well, the aromatic mix of oil, gas, sweat and sheet metal being bent does it for me. It reminds me of how hard a worker you were, of all the things you did and, well, it reminds me of you.

The truck got old and worn down. There were some dings, dents and rust spots, and even a few holes. You found ways to make it usable even then – at least on the property.

When you got sick, you started talking about selling it for the parts. Then you got very sick, and the decision of what to do with the truck became ours.

Most people would have shaken their head at even considering purchasing the old vehicle in the shape it was in. After a few conversations, we found a buyer who likes to tinker and redo vehicles – a neighbor who you would have been glad to have it.

The day they came to tow it away I walked outside to put the key in it. When I opened the door, my memory bank was opened wide as the smells hit my nostrils. No, Daddy, I didn't cry. I smiled. I could close my eyes and see you at the wheel pulling into the driveway or toddling down the road to the hardware store to pick something up.

Grief is not always about sadness.

Now, when they came and got the truck, and we watched it being towed away on the dirt road, I have to say, I got a little misty-eyed, and so did Mom. We were sad because, as Mom said, it was like you leaving us. It didn't last long. Because we knew better, but it still ached a little bit.

Love, Becky

PART II: STORIES OF YOU

Dear Daddy,

If I had to pick some of the best stories about you that I have heard or experienced in my life as your daughter, I would turn to your own writings. You shared your thoughts and such.

Your writings have always had a Christian base, which made sense your Christian walk was important to you. So, here are some of the ones that made the most impact on me. Thank you for sharing Jesus with me ... with us ...

Love, Becky

Burning The Candle at Both Ends.

A candle will produce more light if both ends are burning than it will if only one end is lit; but it will last only half as long. If we have only one candle, we must decide whether we need a little light for a long time or a lot of light for a short while. The candle will last even longer if it burns for only part of the time.

The human body is a remarkable piece of God's work. It can complete almost any task it is asked to perform for limited periods of time. However, it must eventually rest. Most of our rest comes during sleep. Many studies have been made of sleep deprivation. They all indicate that, in the long haul, people function better with the proper mix of work and rest. Someone said that "work never hurts anyone." Someone else said that "all work and no play makes Jack a dull boy."

We cannot all rest and work the same way. But for sure, if we are to be all that we can be, we must learn the right combination. Our minds and bodies are gifts from God, but we are responsible for our well-being. What a shame if we burn out before our mission is concluded.

(James Holland)

Learning To Like What We Have to Do

Not long ago I heard a man say, "I can't wait to retire. The minute I qualify for retirement, I will give my keys to my boss and be gone".

If one becomes employed at age twenty-five, and works until normal retirement age, one will have spent over eighty-three thousand hours on one's job. That is about twenty-three percent of one's total time during these forty years.

Some will not be able to make a living doing what they dreamed about at the onset; they may not enjoy what they must do. If they do not like what they spend so much of their life doing, they may be like the man who couldn't wait to retire. Feelings of discontent may deform their minds that they may not be good fathers, good mothers, good husbands, good wives, good citizens, or good at whatever they do.

Part of the productivity problems in our economy may be traced to the multitude of people who "cannot wait" for, quitting time, Friday, and retirement.

God gave all of us the ability to alter our thinking: therefore, we can learn to adapt to most situations. If one cannot always do what one likes, one and those one's life touches might fare much better, if one learned to like what one has to do.

(James Holland)

Now I Know

Nearly 24 years ago, a parolee of our justice system came into our office and hit my wife on her head with a broken brick. He fractured her skull in two places; she suffered blunt force trauma in at least five others. From the blood spattered over the walls and pooled on the floor, he may have thought that he had killed her; I thought that he surely had tried. When I found her, she could not tell me what had happened. I feared that she would not live to get to a hospital. I only knew to call for help and to hold her. I searched my soul for some kind of solace. Calling upon God seemed to be my only choice. Life was not always without trouble, but I had never dealt with so pressing possibilities.

Over the years, I have voiced consolation to those who had need. I may even have said, "I feel for you". Now I know that I could not possibly have felt their pain. And more than once, for trouble of equal weight, I have recommended a special trust in the Creator, but I could not have known, by experience, that it would have helped. I had been introduced to Christianity over fifty years ago. I had used my faith to find mental peace at more than one time of anxiety, but none as severe as that bad happening. I had come to a place in time when I knew that, with all the personal power I could muster, I could not alter one cell in the hurt body of my beloved partner. I remember asking God to help, but I also remember acknowledging the terrible prospect, and telling Him I would understand. With that said, the assurance came to mind quickly, and then I knew that the promises I had read in the Bible were true. Even though I walked through the valley of the shadow death for one so dear to me, He was there.

After spending several weeks in two hospitals, we brought her home for the rest of her healing. The bills began to come in. We had not prepared for this kind of circumstance. While we were still in the hospital room, my eldest daughter asked, "Daddy, how will you pay for all this"? I am not sure what I told her, but by then I had come to understand that there were no boundaries to God's power.

Several New Years have passed since we first felt our calamity, and now I know, how to feel for those who suffer greatly, how to appreciate what was taken for granted, how to thank God for His grace and mercy, and how to trust Him without exception. We have worn the shoes. We could tell many stories about how He helped by using His people to make our lives better than if we had been walking alone. Things are good for us now; I never expected such diverse support, and now I know the great pleasure that comes from trusting His everlasting promises. Where there once was a dark cloud, the sun shines brightly. **(James Holland)**

Chapter Three: Jimbucks : The perfect cup of joe or jim
Dear Daddy,

We live in coffee world. We have personalized coffee mugs. We have staff meetings just as an excuse to drink more coffee. We don't have paychecks- we work for coffee money. The only language our computers understand is Java. And when a coffee shop hits a town, or even a nearby town, boy do we get excited. We live in a coffee world.

You became a true coffee connoisseur when you first went to college at East Texas Baptist College in Marshall. You never really could say why you liked coffee except you just liked the taste of it.

One of our family's favorite stories about you is your love of coffee. For as long as I can remember, you have had a cup of coffee – black.

You discovered how to make the perfect cup of coffee. After a visit to a coffee shop in Americus, Georgia, called Café Campesino, and seeing their roasting and production process, you caught the coffee bug.

You even made your own coffee maker. It took you a little over a month and half designing the circuitry, but you finally got it made. You have been building things for as long as I can remember. You used old computer parts, plumbing parts and scrap lumber, and the trim was hand-fashioned and individually installed out of pure copper.

You polished the trim with lemon juice and table salt. I remember watching you work on it, and wonder why you were doing it, especially when you could go buy a coffee maker at Walmart for less than $15.

You told me you just wanted a good cup of coffee. "I can have a cup of coffee shop quality coffee," I remember you saying, "without going to the coffee shop." We called the machine 'Jimbucks.'

Then of course, there was the time you built your own coffee roaster. I think that will be a shrine to your creativity.

There are a lot of things out there that you have built that should be a shrine to not just your creativity but your resourcefulness and intelligence. Just ask our water well guy what he found after coming to fix it. He asked to take the part you had created home, so he could study how you made it work.

Thank you, Daddy, for encouraging creativity in us, and for sharing your creativity with us. I miss you.

Love, Becky

Chapter Four: The Day the Church Burned Down

Dear Daddy,

One of the most interesting stories to me about you was when the original Empire Baptist Church burned down in Empire, Georgia. It was your hometown church.

And you burned it down. Dear readers, he didn't do it on purpose. It just happened.

Writer's Note to Readers: *Daddy was a young married man then. He had gone to the church one chilly night to get it ready for the Bible study meeting that was going to be held that night. He had turned the heaters on and had gone up the street to visit some church members who had not been in a while to invite them to the Bible study.*

Daddy, it happened so quickly, and the whole community came out to stop it, but there was nothing much that could be done but to let it burn to the ground when it happened.

No one blamed you for it.

In fact, that very night, you all started the rebuild quickly.

God has always been an important part of your life, and church too. You told me that night changed you. In fact, there were several things over the years that God used to change you – change your prayer habits and the way you saw things.

Grief sucks. As I think and feel the feelings of your loss, I catch myself wondering what you would say or do to help us through it, and I think about the church burning. It was a big loss.

But that didn't stop you or the others from having church – you met in homes, you met in the basement of the lodge and other places while building the new church.

Your loss is a big one for us. But as I know you would tell us, and I mentioned before in a previous letter, we are going to keep on living.

But we might still cry occasionally because you are gone.
And that is OK.

Love Becky

Cranberry Juice Statistics.

Thirty plus years ago, I was advised by my doctor to have a stone removed from my gall bladder. Since a tetanus shot is a major medical procedure to me, I chose to live with the stone. As I dealt with the aggravation, someone told me that cranberry juice would help the stone production problem. Eager to prevent surgery, I drank a small glass of it each day for all those years. Recently, while having a sonogram for another problem, we looked at the gall bladder and found no evidence of stones. I immediately thought of all that red juice, and how it must have helped my problem. As I tried to validate its usefulness, I also discovered that, since I started drinking the juice of the cranberry, we haven't had to replace a single muffler on any of our automobiles.

(James Holland)

Christianity And Lifestyles.

I grew up believing that the salvation that I am confident that I have, came as a gift from a merciful God. I further believe that, at my best, I was and am sinner enough to be lost, and had it not been for the propitiatory sacrifice of his Son, lost would be my spiritual state.

Some of my friends and I differ, in that they believe that they are saved by not being bad, and that they continue to be saved by continuing to be good. However, our difference does not lessen my faith in my god and my salvation, but I am moved to think about my stance. My first thoughts were to defend "the faith" vehemently, but then I began to think more logically. I know myself well, and I know for sure that I would not trust the goodness of one such as I for my keeping. If that were the case, I would be a terribly anxious man.

As I think in the third dimension, I conclude that one's lifestyle has nothing at all to do with one's Christianity, but that one's Christianity has everything to do with one's lifestyle, and that if one would trust Christ to save one from perdition, surly one can trust him to save one from oneself.

(James Holland)

Chapter Five: Computer Talk

Dear Daddy,

The first time I saw a computer – it was one that you built – a desktop – and I was learning math on it – addition, subtraction – all simple first grade stuff. I was seven years old. Now, I am 53, and up until a few weeks ago, I was still using a computer you had built to do writing and my social media marketing on.

When you discovered computers, you found your niche. You still did your stuff to provide for the family – the contracting work as a plumber, heating/air guy and electrician you had – but you now had something else to pursue as an interest.

And being someone who loved to learn, well, technology and computers seemed right up your alley. You even built a computer right before you got sick. It took a little longer, but you built it. I remember you saying that was all that mattered – the project had been completed.

You always told me it was necessary to start and finish a project before starting another one – though sometimes several projects could be connected.

You could talk computers with the best of them, and you did. I remember as a child going to a couple of computer shows with you and watching you hold your own with some of the experts in the field. I don't remember meeting them, but I have been told at one of the computer shows we went to in the early 1970s, Steve (Jobs) and Bill (Gates) were there – novices in the field as it was something new.

Had it not been for your interest and knowledge of computers, my career as a writer may not have flourished in the different outlets that it did. I appreciate that, Daddy.

Grief sucks. As I wrote that sentence, it hit me. You are not here to help me with this project.

No goal on this project really, Daddy. Just writing to share my own experience with loss, while in the midst of it. I can hear you now. Just write it. Sit down, allow sometime and write it.

So, I am.

Thank goodness for you and your computer interest, and computer talks you would have with me.

Love, Becky

Epilogue/Conclusion

Dear Daddy,

      Earl Grollman is credited with saying "Grief is not a disorder, a disease or a sign of weakness. It is an emotional, physical, and spiritual necessity, the price you pay for love. The only cure for grief is to grieve."

      I have talked to several people since you died, and everyone has a different opinion or words to say about the grief process.

      But the one thing they do agree on is. It is OK to grieve.

      Thankfully, as a youngster, you turned your life over to Christ at a church meeting. You were baptized, and you believed that God sent Jesus to die for us and allowed Him to be buried and rise again for us. You and Mom made sure that you set your marriage and our home on a solid Christian foundation.

      Because though we can be sad and miss you, we can celebrate that you are in your Heavenly Home with Jesus.

      Grief sucks. It does.

      I miss you, Daddy. We all do.

      Love, Becky

Resources

My Jesus – Heartache to Hope, by Anne Wilson

Like a River - Finding the Faith and Strength to Move Forward after Loss and Heartache by Granger Smith

The Holy Bible

Acknowledgments

Thank you to God for the grace, mercy, unconditional love and peace He has given us, and for the chance to share this project.

Thank you to our friends, family and neighbors, especially those in Cochran and Empire, Georgia, for your love, prayers and support.

Bridges That We Never Cross.

Worry is at times futuristic. Many of our fears come to haunt us as we consider possibilities. Sometimes our energy and intelligence are wasted as we speculate that our worst fears will come to pass.

Our transportation used to be by horse drawn wagons; some of the horses were afraid to cross bridges. Now and then, they would bolt and run.

When we traveled, we missed much of the pleasure of the trip while worrying that there might be a bridge in our way. Many times, we reached our destination without ever encountering one.

Bridges that we never cross, may have more to do with our mental ease than the bridges of reality.

(James Holland)

Capable of Compassion

Forty-five years ago, my wife and I left our home in Dodge County, Georgia to seek our fortune at a college in Marshall, Texas. We had built a little house on an acre of land that I had purchased as a teenager, and we had planned to make our life in that place. We had been married for less than two years, when we decided that I needed to go to college. A family friend was vice president of a small Baptist school in the piney woods of east Texas, and he had invited us to do our college work there. We were just on the upper side of twenty years; we were young and gutsy. We sold our house and purchased a mobile home, we called them house trailers back then, and pulled it eight hundred miles to a town that we knew very little about.

We arrived in town with what we thought was enough money to get our "trailer" set up and ready for our new adventure. We felt sure that we could spend what we had, fully knowing that shortly my severance check from the job that I had left would come. When the check did not come, and when we had spent most of our monies, I began looking for some kind of work. We learned to eat pinto beans and day-old bread to keep the cost of groceries down. One could buy a large bag of dried beans for not much, and we could eat from them for several days. All Texans ate a lot of beans, and we had learned to prepare them more than one way. There was a bakery in town. We reasoned that most bread that we bought in a store was a day old before we got it anyway, so we bought our bread at the surplus store. The costs of getting the "trailer' set up was much more than we had planned, and our money ran out. Here we were, two inexperienced young people in a town with no family, there wasn't a relative in the whole state.

This was a college town, and there were more people than there were jobs. We were not hungry, we still had beans and day-old bread. We had a roof over our heads, but since the check had not come, I had to look for work.

I knew that there wasn't much gasoline in the car, but I felt that there was enough to go across town to apply for a job that I had heard about. I had placed a rifle, that I had bought before we got married, in the car a few days earlier, thinking that, when I could get the courage, I would sell it or pawn it. I never got the courage, so the rifle was still in the car.

On the way back to our "trailer" the car ran out of gas. I began to get anxious. The car had stopped on a narrow bridge over some railroad tracks. When I had determined that it was indeed out of fuel, I picked up the rifle and walked to a nearby service station to see if I could trade it for one gallon of gasoline, gas was selling in Texas then for twenty cents a gallon. I only wanted enough to get the car home. I recognized the station owner as a member of a church we attended. I told him of my dilemma. He wasn't very polite. He said that he didn't need a rifle, and that he wasn't into credit or charity, I had not asked for either. I started back toward the car, feeling low, I did not know how I was to get it off the narrow bridge. I heard someone call from behind. I looked and saw a man walking toward me with a container that had enough gas to get the car started. When we had it running, I drove him back to the station and he asked me to pull up to the gas pump, where he pumped ten gallons into my empty tank, pulled two dollars from his own pocket and paid the owner of the station. I offered him the same rifle that his boss would not trade for one gallon of fuel, but he would not take it. He said, "I have been in trouble too." A few days later our check arrived and I drove to the station to pay him the two dollars. He would not take it until I insisted.

Marshall was a real college town. There was a black Methodist college, a black Baptist college and the all white college that I was to attend. There were no outward racial troubles, but there wasn't much racial togetherness either. The "blacks" lived on one side of town and the "whites" lived on the other.

I already knew that the tensions between the races, that I had seen growing up, were not right, and I had made my mind up to rid prejudice from my being. That experience, when my car ran out of gas and a young black service station attendant came to a white Georgia boy's aid, helped me to know that all people can exercise the kind of compassion that our loving God intended.

(James Holland)

About the Author

Rebecca Holland, or Becky as she is called, is a retired 20-year, award-winning veteran newspaper journalist, and published author. She received her bachelor's degree and master's degree from the University of West Alabama in Livingston and has had her work published in more than two dozen print and online publications in Texas, Georgia and Alabama. Her hobbies include reading, photography, flower gardening and watching football.